Fingerpower®

Level Three

Effective Technic for All Piano Methods

By John W. Schaum

Edited by Wesley Schaum

FOREWORD

Strong fingers are an important requirement for all pianists, amateur and professional. Schaum Fingerpower® exercises are designed to strengthen all five fingers of both hands.

Equal hand development is assured by the performance of the same patterns in each hand. The exercises are short and easily memorized. This enables the student to focus his/her efforts on technical benefits, listening attentively, and playing with a steady beat.

A measure number (enclosed in a small box) is included at the beginning of each system of music. This makes it easier to locate measures during the lesson and for written practice assignments.

The exercises become progressively more difficult as the student moves through the book. This makes the exercises an ideal companion to a method book at the same level.

The series consists of seven books, Primer Level through Level 6.

To access audio, visit:
www.halleonard.com/mylibrary

Enter Code
3904-8893-6452-9238

ISBN 978-1-936098-93-4

I0792513

Exclusively Distributed By
HAL•LEONARD®
7777 W. Bluemound Rd. P.O. Box 13819 Milwaukee, WI 53213

CONTENTS

PRACTICE SUGGESTIONS

To derive the full benefit from these exercises, they should be played with a firm, solid finger action. **Listen carefully while practicing**. Try to play **each finger equally loud**. Each hand should also play equally loud. It is also important to be aware of the feeling in your fingers and hands during practice.

Each exercise should be practiced four or five times daily, starting at a slow tempo and gradually increasing the tempo as proficiency improves. Several previously learned exercises should be reviewed each week as part of regular practice.

ABOUT THE AUDIO

To access the accompanying audio, go to **www.halleonard.com/mylibrary** and enter the code found on the first page of this book. This will grant you instant access to every example.

There are two tracks for each exercise:

1. Slow practice tempo
2. Performance tempo

The solo part is emphasized on the practice track. The accompaniment is emphasized on the performance track. There are two extra count-in measures before each track.

Follow these three steps for practice variety. At first, the steps should be done with the slow practice tempo. The same steps may be used again at the performance tempo.

1. Student plays right hand only
2. Student plays left hand only
3. Student plays both hands together

1. Triplets

2. Two Notes Against One (R.H.)

3. Two Notes Against One (L.H.)

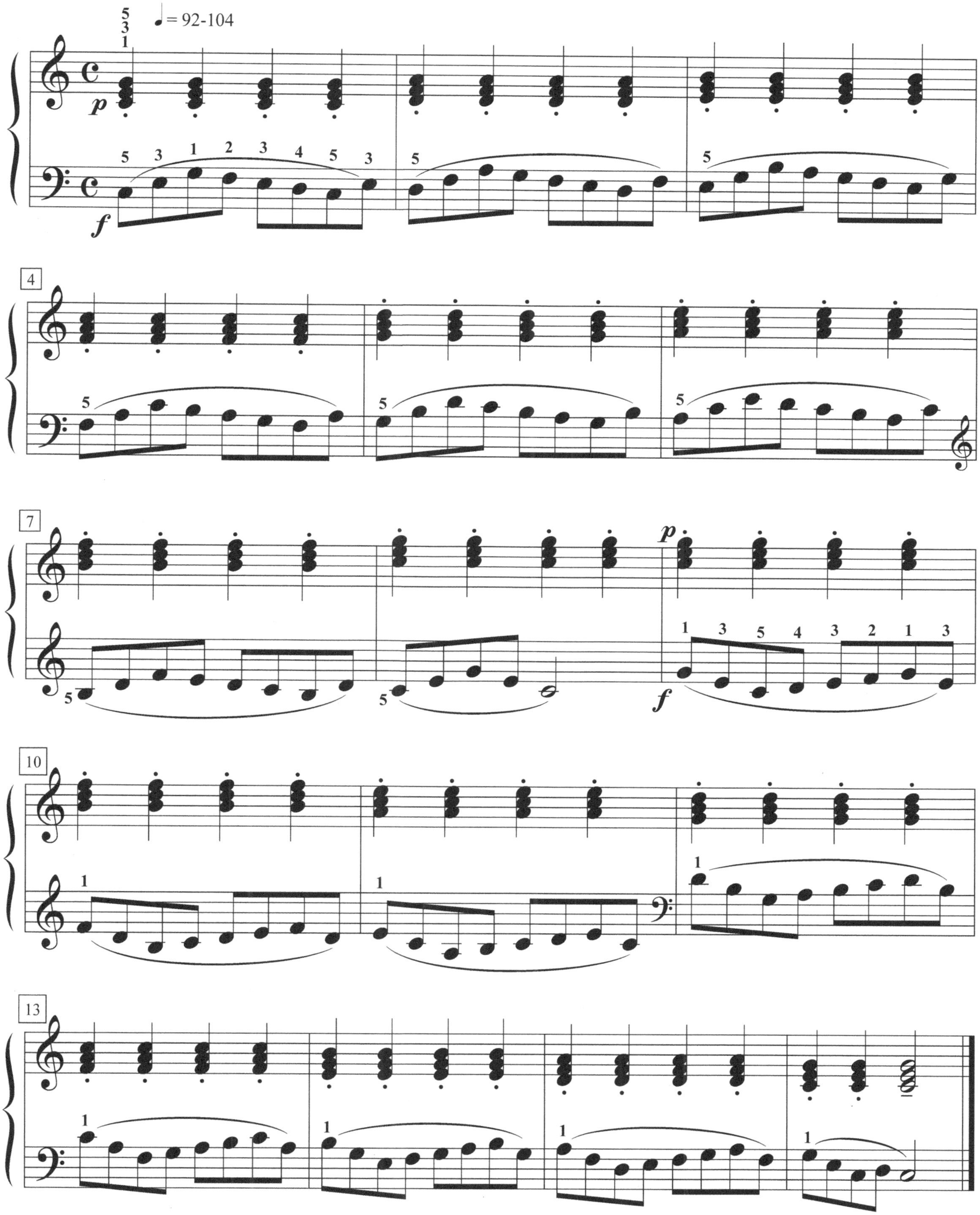

4. Cross Hand Etude (3/4)

5. Cross Hand Etude (4/4)

6. Chord Inversions

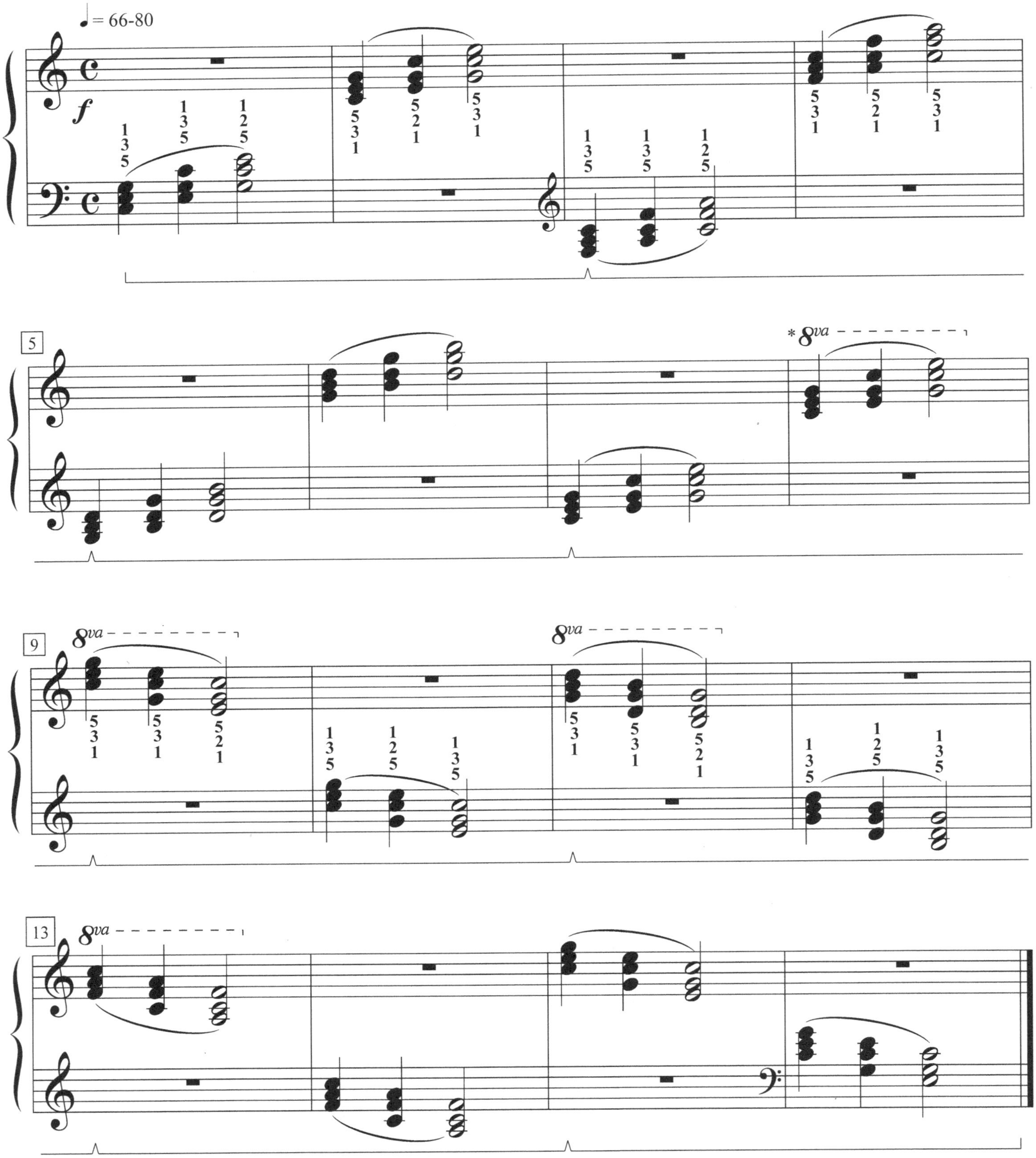

*8va = play one octave HIGHER than written.

7. Hand Stretching Technique

8. Finger Velocity

*9. Sustaining the Thumb

* Be sure that all whole notes played by the thumb are held down for ***four full counts***.

*10. Sustaining the Second Finger

* Be sure that all whole notes played by the 2nd finger are held down for ***four full counts***.

*11. Sustaining the Third Finger

* Be sure that all dotted half notes played by the 3rd finger are held down for ***three full counts.***

*12. Sustaining the Fourth Finger

* Be sure that all whole notes played by the 4th finger are held down for ***four full counts.***

*13. Sustaining the Fifth Finger

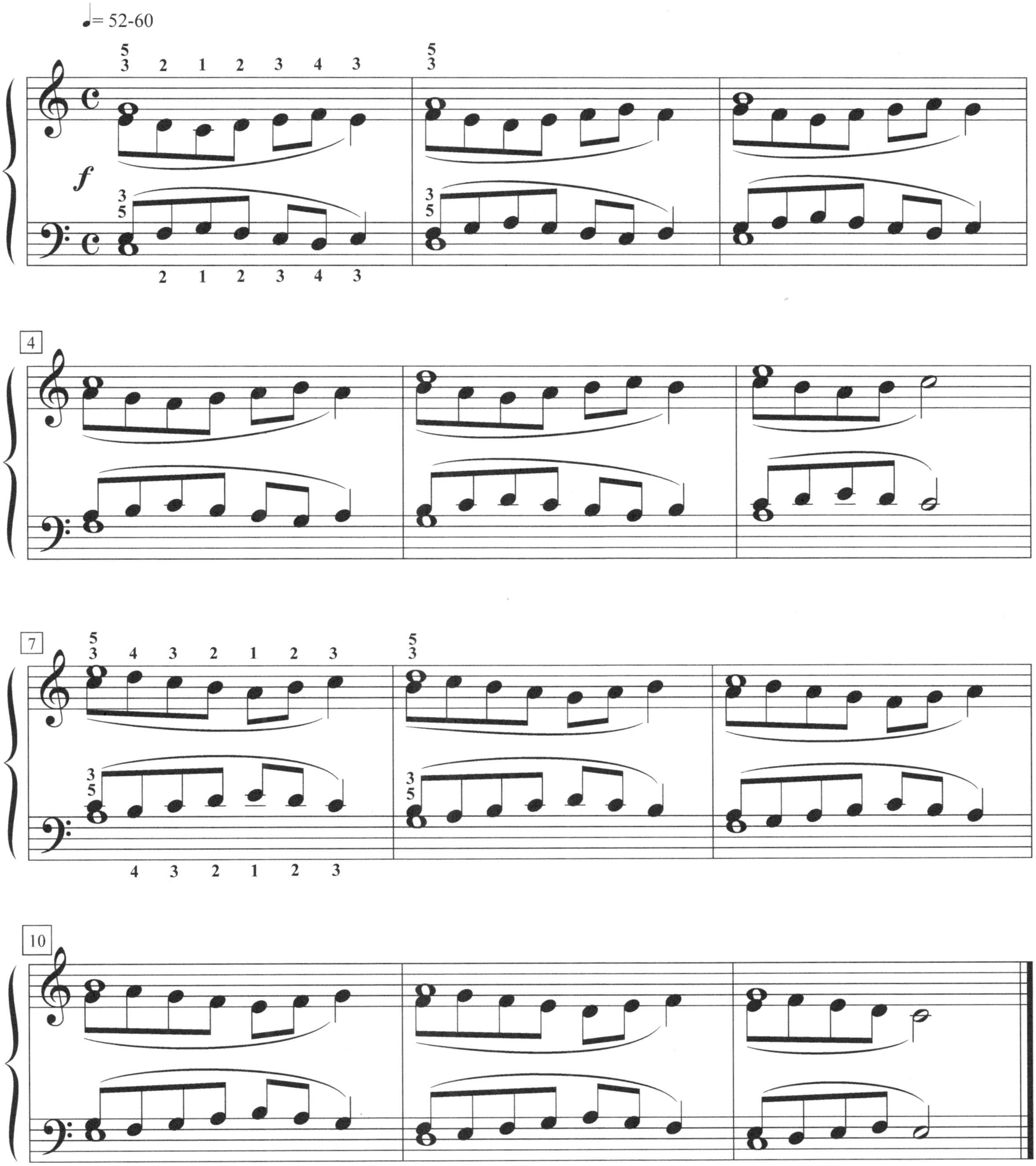

* Be sure that all whole notes played by the 5th finger are held down for ***four full counts.***

14. Scale Passages and Staccato Chords

15. Legato Thirds

*16. Dotted Eighth and Sixteenth Notes

* The rhythm for the dotted 8th and 16th must be ***played accurately***. Be careful that it is ***not*** played like an 8th note triplet.

17. Etude For the Weaker Fingers

18. Interlocking Hand Pattern

19. Chromatic Chord Etude

20. Chromatic Arpeggio Etude

17
R.H. over
L.H.
20
R.H. over
L.H.
23
26
29